MARVEL

D0204368

 phoenix international publications, inc.

In New York City, there are so many workers who help keep things in order. But when chaos breaks out, it's Spider-Man to the rescue!

While Spidey and Friends fight off the bad guys, search the streets for these civil servants:

this letter carrier

this construction worker

this street vendor

this police officer

this firefighter

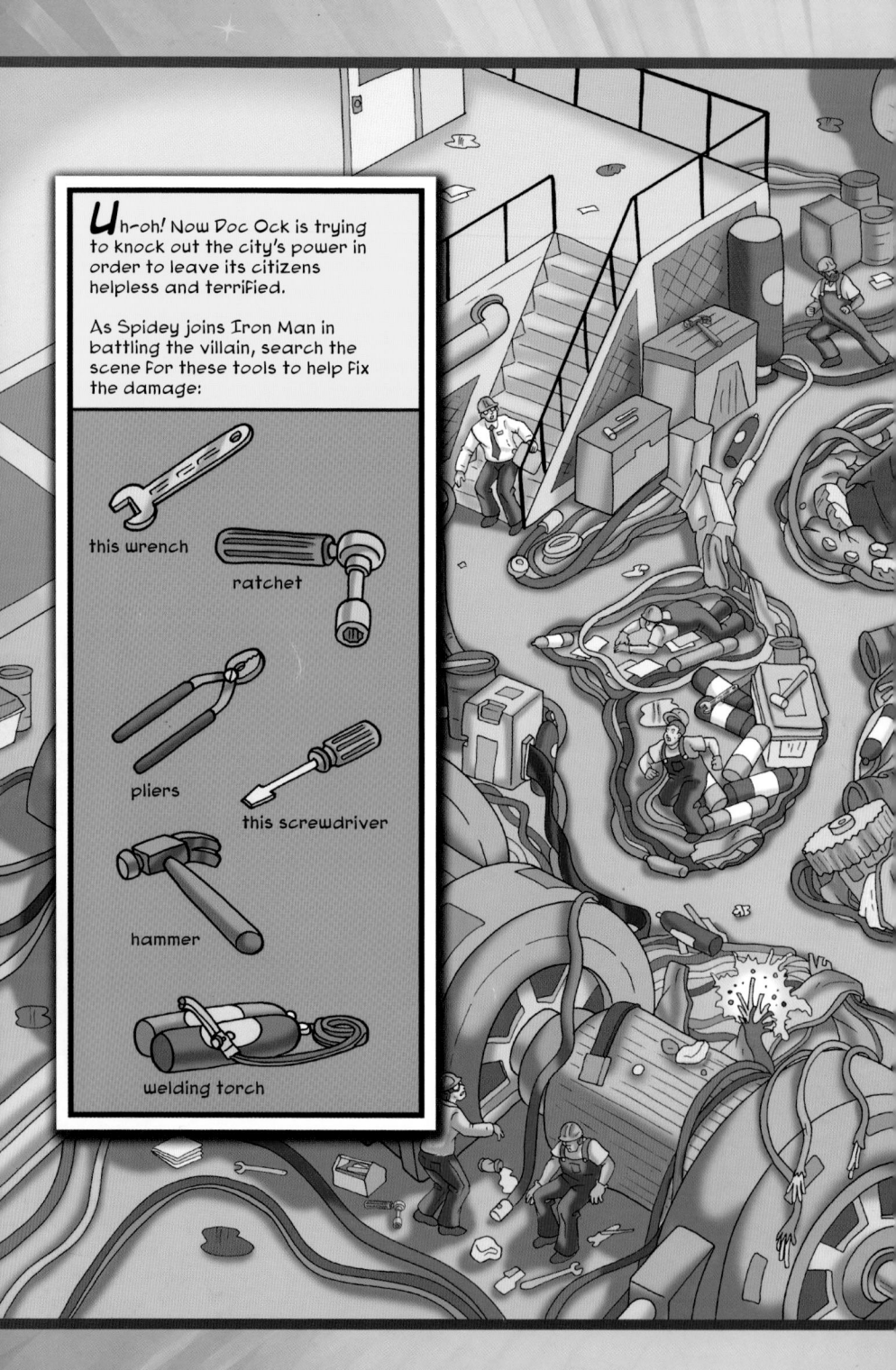

Uh-oh! Now Doc Ock is trying to knock out the city's power in order to leave its citizens helpless and terrified.

As Spidey joins Iron Man in battling the villain, search the scene for these tools to help fix the damage:

this wrench

ratchet

pliers

this screwdriver

hammer

welding torch

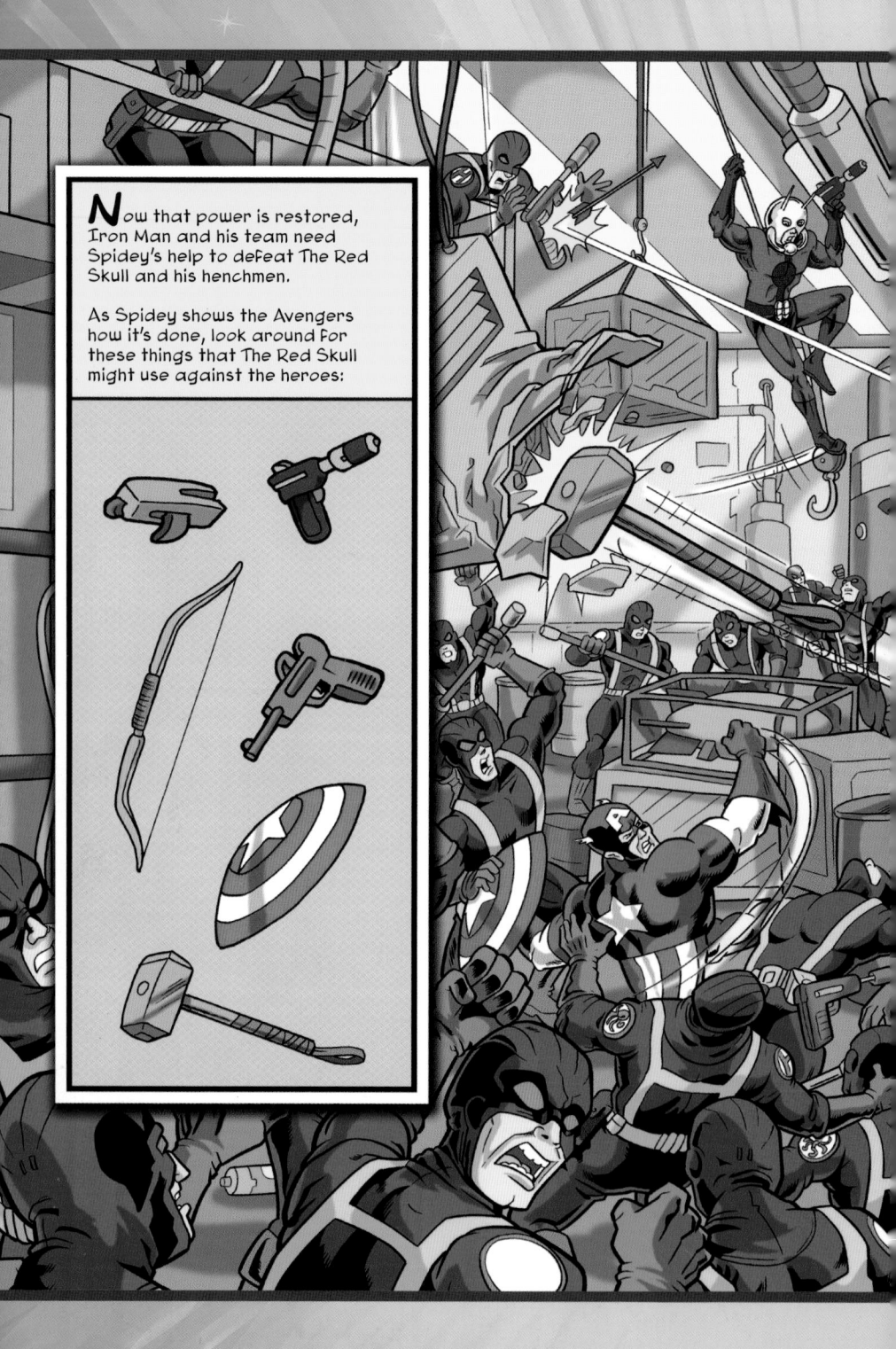

Now that power is restored, Iron Man and his team need Spidey's help to defeat The Red Skull and his henchmen.

As Spidey shows the Avengers how it's done, look around for these things that The Red Skull might use against the heroes:

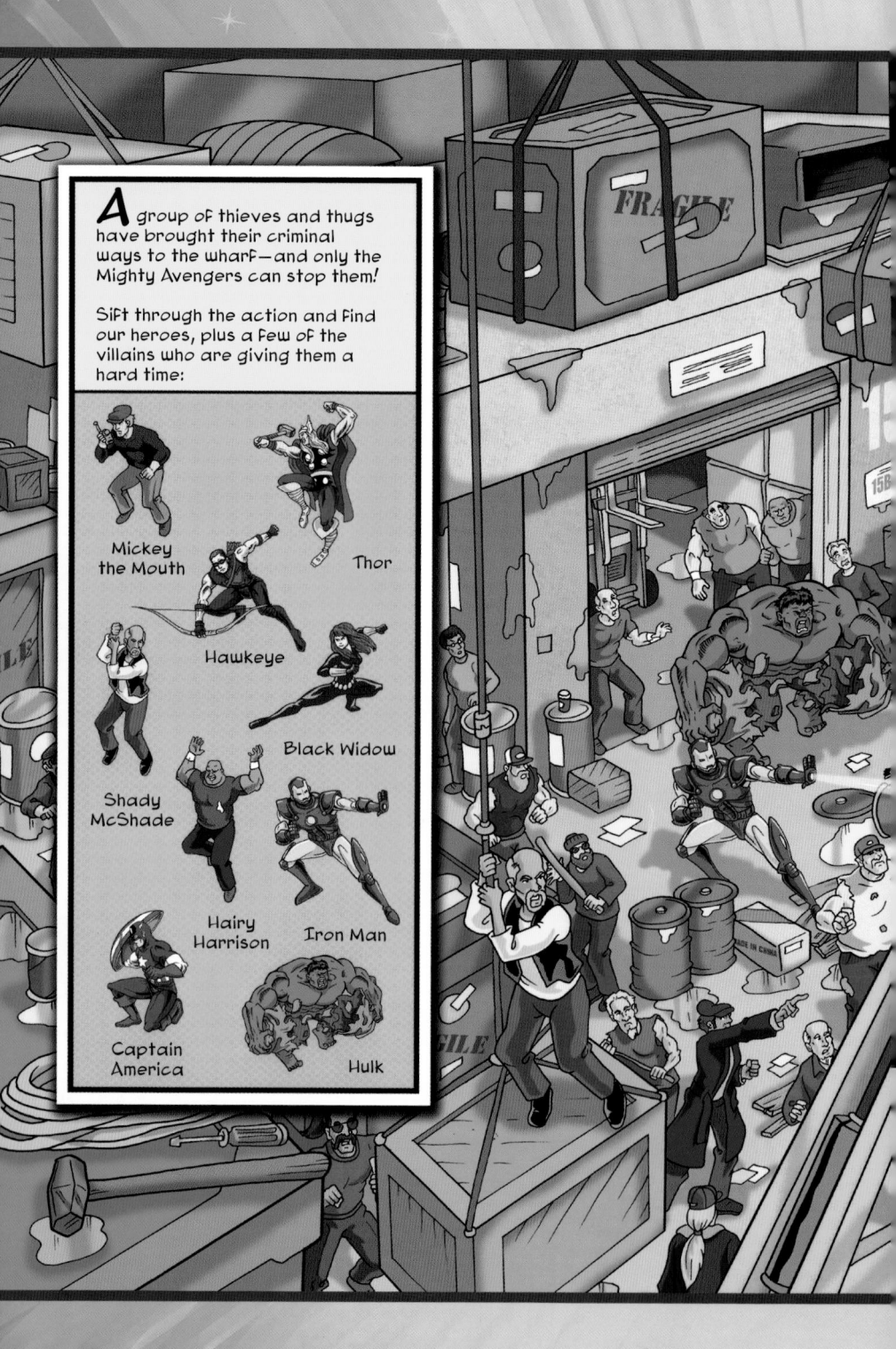

It's a beautiful day at Metro Beach, but The Leader and The Abomination are ruining it.

Help The Avengers find these folks in need of a hand:

Ghosts and ghouls are on the loose in the graveyard!

As the Avengers fight off evil, look around for these creepy creatures:

this ghost

this vampire

this zombie

this ghost

this goblin

this hand

Thanos is wreaking havoc in The Collector's Museum on Knowhere!

Search the scene for the troublemaker, as well as these Guardians of the Galaxy who have come to the rescue:

Groot

Thanos

Star-Lord

Drax

Rocket

Gamora

Now Xandar is under attack! The Guardians of the Galaxy arrive to save the planet and its people from Ronan's evils.

As Star-Lord and Friends battle Ronan's army of aliens, look for these spaceships:

Return to the big city and find these traffic signs on the bustling and chaotic streets:

Go back below ground to NYC's power grid center and find these 6 electricians:

Hurry back to Spidey's battle against The Red Skull and search for 6 Hydra logos.

Wander back to the wharf and find these things lurking in and around the docks:

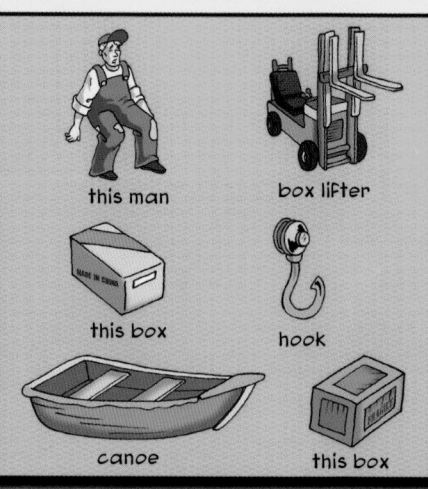

this man

box lifter

this box

hook

canoe

this box

Boogie back to the beach and find this sandy summer stuff:

- sandcastle
- flying disc
- volleyball
- bucket and shovel
- sunscreen
- surf board

Creep back to the graveyard and find these goofy tombstone markings:

NOAH
MOORE
IS NO MORE

DAISY
PUSHING

HAMLET
GOOD NIGHT
SWEET PRINCE

THIS
BLOKE
WENT UP
IN SMOKE

Silly Sally
held her breath
and now
she's breathed
her last

SHERRY CHERRY
Choked on a
chokecherry

Cruise back to The Collector's Museum and find Cosmo, plus these collectibles that could help the Guardians defeat Thanos:

Cosmo

Fight your way back to the Guardians' epic battle against Ronan and find these evil aliens: